100+ Fun Ideas for
Practising Modern Foreign Languages

in the Primary Classroom

Activities for developing Oracy and
Literacy skills

Sue Cave

Brilliant
PUBLICATIONS

We hope you and your pupils enjoy the activities in this book. Brilliant Publications publishes many other books for teaching modern foreign languages. To find out more details on any of the titles listed below, please log onto our website: www.brilliantpublications.co.uk.

More Fun Ideas for Advancing Modern Foreign Languages in the Primary Classroom	978-1-905780-72-3
Chantez Plus Fort!	978-1-903853-37-5
Hexagonie 1	978-1-905780-59-4
Hexagonie 2	978-1-905780-18-1
Jouons Tous Ensemble	978-1-903853-81-8
C'est Français!	978-1-903853-02-3
J'aime Chanter!	978-1-905780-11-2
J'aime Parler!	978-1-905780-12-9
French Pen Pals Made Easy	978-1-905780-10-5
Loto Français	978-1-905780-45-7
French Festivals and Traditions	978-1-905780-44-0
Bonne Idée	978-1-905780-62-4
Unforgettable French	978-1-905780-54-9
¡Es Español!	978-1-903853-64-1
Juguemos Todos Juntos	978-1-903853-95-5
¡Vamos a Cantar!	978-1-905780-13-6
Spanish Pen Pals Made Easy	978-1-905780-42-3
Lotto en Español	978-1-905780-47-1
Spanish Festivals and Traditions	978-1-905780-53-2
Buena Idea	978-1-905789-63-1
Das ist Deutsch	978-1-905780-15-0
Wir Spielen Zusammen	978-1-903853-97-9
German Pen Pals Made Easy	978-1-905780-43-3
Deutsch-Lotto	978-1-905780-46-4
German Festivals and Traditions	978-1-905780-52-5
Gute Idee	978-1-905780-65-5
Giochiamo Tutti Insieme	978-1-903853-96-2
Lotto in Italiano	978-1-905780-48-8
Buon'Idea	978-1-905780-64-8

Acknowledgement

Thank you very much to the pupils and staff at Farley Hill Primary School for allowing us to take the photos used in this book.

Written by Sue Cave. Copyright © Sue Cave 2006
Cover and inside illustrations by Lynda Murray
Photos by Julie Thatcher. Photos copyright © Julie Thatcher 2006
Front cover designed by Brilliant Publications

Printed ISBN: 978-1-903853-98-6
ebook ISBN: 978-0-85747-124-6

Printed in the UK.
First published 2006, reprinted 2007, 2008, 2009, 2010

10 9 8   7   6   5

Published by Brilliant Publications
Unit 10
Sparrow Hall Farm
Edlesborough
Dunstable
Bedfordshire
LU6 2ES, UK

E-mail: info@brilliantpublications.co.uk
Website: www.brilliantpublications.co.uk
Tel: 01525 222292

Contents

Preface

This resource book is a compilation of tried and tested ideas for practising a foreign language in the primary classroom. The ideas for the activities are ones which I have devised, collected or adapted during the last ten years as a peripatetic language specialist in primary schools. I recommend them due to the response I have received from young learners and the positive impact the activities have had on their learning of another language. It is hoped that by collating these activities under one cover, they will be easily accessible for the busy teacher.

The inherent rationale behind each activity is that it is interactive, communicative, memorable and enjoyable. The most popular activities in this book invariably include at least one 'key ingredient', namely:

✦ manipulation
✦ a shared secret
✦ competition
✦ surprise
✦ physical movement

These ingredients make up a recipe for success!

Very few resources are needed other than the teacher, the children, paper, card and items often found in a primary school classroom. The ideas could be used as stand-alone activities throughout the school week as reinforcement of language previously encountered or as an integral part of a longer language teaching session. They are suitable for a wide variety of topics and for most modern foreign languages. Repetition and practice are essential in language learning; the variety of activities suggested in this book should provide plenty of opportunity for this.

For each resource, I have suggested ideas to develop both oracy and literacy skills. At the start of each section you will find codes relating to the oracy and literacy objectives in the 'Key Stage 2 Framework for Languages'. There are activities related to many of these objectives across the four years in Key Stage 2. For a complete list of how the activities relate to the objectives, refer to the table in the introduction.

I hope that you have fun using and perhaps adapting these ideas in the teaching of a foreign language to your young learners. I certainly have done and continue to do so.

Sue Cave
April 2006

Introduction

Team games and competition

Many of the ideas and activities in this book suggest how a competitive element can be included. I have found that competition encourages children to participate more readily and with even greater enthusiasm than they might do otherwise. Children who seem to be reticent or appear to lack confidence in using a foreign language in the classroom, often join in with a game with relish. This seems to be true for many boys, in particular. Team games take away the emphasis from the individual. They allow children to learn, perform and develop skills in the 'safe' environment of a group of peers.

I avoid single sex teams but try to orchestrate mixed ability teams. These teams are normally organized on a teaching session basis and new ones formed in the next lesson. However, you could keep the same teams and develop a 'league' to which points are added after each game.

As in any competition, rules are essential to ensure the smooth running and fairness of the game. I tell the children that the teacher is the referee and the 'ref's' decision is final! I allow the winning team to perform a victory salute and announce that they are the 'Champions!' in the target language. This is a privilege given only to the winners which is much respected and esteemed by all.

Team games are always popular. The children become so engrossed that they are oblivious to the amount of repetition taking place. You might guess from all this, that I like team games and find them an effective strategy in language learning. However, if you feel that it would be more appropriate for your class to learn in a less competitive atmosphere, the majority of the activities can be played just as well without explicit competition.

Key Stage 2 Framework for Languages Objectives

Objective	Activity number
O3.1	1, 2, 40, 114, 115, 116
O3.2	42, 62, 63, 67, 77, 117, 120
O3.3	8, 9, 10, 11, 12, 13, 14, 15, 16, 17, 34, 35, 36, 46, 47, 48, 50, 56, 57, 58, 59, 60, 76, 79, 80, 81, 82, 83, 85, 86, 87, 105, 106, 107, 108
O3.4	3, 4, 5, 6, 7, 44, 45, 65, 67, 68, 69, 70, 71, 72, 73, 74, 75, 76, 84
L3.1	19, 20, 24, 27, 98, 109
L3.2	30
L3.3	39, 100, 101
O4.1	118, 120
O4.2	44, 45
O4.3	41, 43, 67
O4.4	18, 31, 32, 37, 49, 61, 63, 64, 78, 88, 89, 90, 91, 92, 94, 95, 96, 97
L4.1	22, 23, 29, 103, 104, 109
L4.2	21, 25, 26, 28, 113
L4.3	102
L4.4	39, 54, 103, 104, 125, 129
O5.1	31, 51
O5.2	33, 89, 93
O5.4	119, 121, 122, 123, 124
L5.2	66, 99, 110, 111, 112
L5.3	55, 103, 104, 126, 127, 128, 130, 131
O6.2	38, 51, 52, 53, 119, 121, 124
L6.1	135, 137
L6.4	132, 133, 134, 135, 136, 137

Flashcards

Flashcards are an excellent way of bypassing the mother tongue and encouraging the use of the target language. They are very versatile and can be used in many activities.

Flashcards can easily be made from images, either hand-drawn, collected from magazines, or using 'clipart' obtained either online or from commercially produced software. Home-produced images need to be strengthened with card and laminating will increase their durability. The flashcards can be colour coded as a prompt for remembering the gender of nouns. Alternatively, coloured stickers could be used.

A5 size is normally big enough for all to see in a classroom. Smaller cards are better for group work.

Year 3 children playing 'Match the word to the image'

Oracy

O3.1, O3.3, O3.4, O4.4

In the following activities, flashcards provide cues for oral repetition, simple communicative tasks and demonstrating recognition.

Responding to rhymes, stories and songs

1. Listen and show

✦ Create images on cards which relate to key words and sounds in rhymes, stories and songs.

✦ Distribute the cards amongst the children and then ask them to raise the cards showing the corresponding image as the words are recited in the story, song or rhyme.

2. Card sequencing

✦ Put the children in groups.

✦ Give the children small versions of the cards from activity 1, relating to key words and sounds in rhymes, stories and songs.

✦ Ask them to sequence the cards as they hear them.

Listening, recognizing and responding to sounds and words

3. **Point to a card**

✦ Position the cards around the room.

✦ Say a word and then ask the children to point to the correct image.

✦ The children love it when you speed up this activity and keep repeating the same word or sound in succession.

4. **Clap if true**

✦ Show a card and say a word.

✦ If the word matches the card, the children either clap, say 'true', stand up or nod, etc.

✦ This is a good game to play competitively, with the children versus the teacher, awarding a point to the teacher if the children clap at the wrong time. This encourages intense listening, as the children always want to beat the teacher!

5. **Splat!**

✦ Stick the flashcards for a given topic on the board.

✦ Divide the class into two teams and ask a repesentative from each team to come to the board.

✦ Say a word or sound, and the first person to 'splat' the corresponding card, wins a point.

✦ This is always a popular game which never has a lack of willing volunteers.

✦ Hint: A useful rule here is 'the first touch is the only touch.'

6. Say and show

✦ Prepare sets of small versions of flashcards.

✦ Divide the children into teams of four or five, and give each team a set of cards.

✦ Ask the children to arrange the cards on the table so that everyone can reach them.

✦ Say a word or sound, and the first group to hold up the correct image wins a point.

7. Picture bingo

✦ Give each table of children several copies of the images for a given topic and ask the children to choose four or five images each or between two. This number of images keeps each game reasonably short and allows it to be played several times, ensuring several winners.

✦ I normally suggest that they work in pairs for this so as to feel supported.

✦ Tell them that when they hear the word or sound, they should turn over the correct image.

✦ When they have turned over all their images, they should shout the equivalent of 'Bingo!' in the target language.

Practising language using single words or phrases

8. Strange voices

✦ Using a visual image on a card as a prompt, ask the children to say the word or phrase slowly, quickly, quietly, loudly, sadly, in a strange voice, etc.

✦ As you can imagine, being allowed to say a word or phrase very loudly is very appealing to most children. Interestingly, in the same way, so is quietly.

9. Numbered cards

✦ Once the children know some numbers in the target language, stick flashcards onto a whiteboard and write a number next to each one.

✦ Call out a number in the target language and the children say the word for the picture on the flashcard.

10. **Guess the card**

✦ This is a popular game which involves a lot of repetition without becoming tedious, and can be used to reinforce new vocabulary.

✦ Put the children into teams.

✦ Jumble up about eight flashcards and hold them with the images facing you and away from the children.

✦ One child from the first team guesses what the first card is. If the guess is wrong, the next team has a go and so on, until the correct word is guessed.

✦ Once correctly guessed, display the cards so as to remind them which ones are no longer in the pack. The game continues until no cards remain.

11. **Card above the head**

✦ This is similar to activity 10, but I believe that it is particularly appealing to the children because there is a shared secret, one of the 'key ingredients'.

✦ Ask a child to sit at the front and hold a card above his/her head so s/he cannot see it.

✦ The child has to guess what the image is. The rest of the class says if the guess is correct or not.

✦ To make it more challenging, you can restrict the number of attempts.

12. **Slow reveal**

✦ Slowly reveal one card at a time from behind a box or out of a bag.

✦ Ask the children to produce the word or phrase as quickly as possible once they recognize it.

13. **Quick flash**

✦ Once the children are familiar with the images and words, literally, 'flash' a card quickly so that the children barely see it.

✦ You'll be amazed at how fast they recognize the image and produce the word.

14. **Snap!**

✦ Make sets of small flashcards with images of recently learnt vocabulary and give one set to each child.

✦ In pairs, the children take it in turns to turn over a card from their pile and say the word or phrase aloud.

✦ When the same image is turned over consecutively, the first child to call out 'Snap!' or its equivalent in the target language, wins both piles of cards that have been turned over so far.

✦ The winner is the child to have the most cards, or all the cards, at the end of an allotted time.

15. **Which is missing?**

✦ Display the flashcards and then ask the children to close their eyes.

✦ Remove a card, then ask the children to open their eyes and say which it is.

16. **Mime a card**

✦ Ask a child to select one of the cards but not to show it to the rest of the class.

✦ The child mimes what was on the card and the other children have to guess what it is.

17. Ask for a card

✦ Children love to be able to handle the cards, in fact any resource (see Realia section) and they tend to be highly motivated in this activity to produce the necessary language in order to be able to hold a card.

✦ Distribute small flashcards amongst the children representing various vocabulary items for a given topic.

✦ Select a willing child who has not got a card to say a word or words in the target language which describes the picture on one of the cards.

✦ The owner of this card hands it over to the child who asked for it. And so the game continues with the cards passing between the children.

✦ Hint: I maintain a fast pace in this activity so that the cards pass through as many hands as possible.

Asking and answering questions

18. **Which card do you have?**

✦ Ask several children to stand at the front of the classroom holding a flashcard facing towards them.

✦ The rest of the class tries to find out who has which card by asking questions such as, 'Do you have…?', 'Do you like…?', 'Is it…?', etc.

✦ The children with the cards can answer with only 'yes' or 'no'.

Literacy

L3.1, L3.2, L4.1, L4.2

Ideally, the sound of words or phrases should be practised first without seeing the written form. This avoids mispronunciation until the children are more secure in their reading skills in the target language. However, it is important that seeing the written word is not delayed too long so that they can begin to link the phonemes to graphemes. Initially, this is a gradual process to familiarize them with words and sounds in the written form.

Once again, the versatility of flashcards means they can be used for activities to develop this skill. In the early stages of language learning, small amounts of language will be presented, thereby making it feasible to show the words or phrases on flashcards. Make word cards to present to the class and practise in chorus. Obviously, they should be in large enough writing or type for the class to be able to read them. Smaller versions of the word cards can also be used in a variety of activities described below.

Reading, recognizing and understanding familiar words in written form

19. Match the word to the image

✦	Create small versions of picture flashcards and provide accompanying cards with the written word. Hand these out to the children.

✦	Ask the children to pair up the word and image so that they match.

✦	This activity works well as a team game. It is amazing how quickly they speed up their ability to read and recognize the word in order to beat the other teams.

20. **Pairs**

✦ Play a game of 'Pairs' using the same cards as in activity 19.

✦ Ask the children to spread the cards out face down and then take it in turns to turn them over two at a time. If the word and image match, the pair is kept.

✦ The winner is the child with the most pairs at the end.

21. **Order the words**

✦ Provide each child or pair with a set of cards with a word or phrase on each.

✦ Read out loud a list of words and then ask them to arrange the word cards in that order on the table in front of them.

22. **Make a sentence**

✦　In preparation for a writing activity, provide small cards with words from key phrases.

✦　Ask the children to construct their own sentences for a given topic.

✦　This activity will be familiar to Key Stage 1 teachers, as it is often used to develop English literacy skills.

23. **Join up the words**

✦　Make sets of cards with a word on each, then cut each card in half.

✦　Ask the children to reconstruct the words by putting together the two halves correctly.

✦　Less able children could be given a set of cards with the written word superimposed on the corresponding image.

24. **Dictionary order**

◆ To practise dictionary skills, ask the children to sort the cards into dictionary order according to the first letter of each word.

◆ This works well as a timed team game.

25. **Read and show**

◆ This is similar to activity 1. Distribute the key word cards for a story, rhyme or song and ask the children to hold up the appropriate word card as it is heard.

26. **Word bingo**

◆ Provide cards with words rather than images (as in activity 7) and ask each child or pair to choose three or four words from a set.

◆ Call out the words. If a child has that word, s/he turns over the card.

◆ When a child has turned over all his/her words, s/he calls out 'Bingo!' in the appropriate way in the target language.

◆ Hint: To save card, when making smaller sets of cards, I place the image on one side and the word on the other.

27. **Word sequence**

◆ For vocabulary which follows a definite sequence, such as months or days of the week, provide teams of children with sets of cards with words written on them.

◆ Mix up the cards and then ask the children to race against each other to arrange the words in the correct order.

28. **Verbal dominoes**

✦ This activity requires a little bit of organization and explanation but once the children understand what they have to do, it is very effective in giving them practice in recognizing and reading words.

✦ Give each child or pair a piece of paper divided like a domino, with a word on each half of it.

✦ Ask one child to start by saying the word on the right-hand side of his/her domino.

✦ The child who has the same word written on the left-hand side of his/her domino, then says the word on the right-hand side.

✦ The activity continues until the first child hears the word written on the left-hand side of his/her domino, which means the game is at an end.

✦ This works very well with numbers written as figures. An even more challenging game is to use questions and answers.

✦ Hint: Keep a record of the order of the words close at hand in case of confusion.

29. **Words in a bag**

✦   Place words written on cards in a bag, ask a child to take out a card, look at it and then invite the other children to guess what the word is.

✦   You could introduce a more competitive element by limiting the number of guesses.

Reading aloud familiar words and making links with phonemes

30. **Spot the phoneme**

✦ To establish a link between phonemes and graphemes, produce groups of flashcards with single words which have the same sound in them. In these words, the grapheme(s) for a specific phoneme should be highlighted in a different colour (only one phoneme highlighted per word).

✦ Use these cards to practise reading in unison.

✦ With smaller versions of these highlighted flashcards, ask the children to group the cards according to similar sounds and coloured phonemes.

Puppets and soft toys

Being able to handle soft toys and puppets is a motivational factor in practising and producing language. Even the most mature primary child can 'melt' at being able to hold a cuddly toy.

Puppets

Puppets provide variety as the character of each can be invented and reinvented to allow for different responses. Interacting with a puppet can seem less intimidating than with an adult or even another child. They can also be used to deliver performances to the rest of the class, school and parents.

Children in years 3 and 4 respond well to puppets. Older children in Key Stage 2 enjoy using puppets to tell a story.

Year 3 children playing 'Puppet fun'

Puppets and soft toys

Children can bring in puppets from home, or make their own from old socks or even paper bags. In addition, you can bring along a selection of puppets, each with its own personality. They will no doubt become familiar and welcome faces in the PMFL classroom. I have a shy bear called Sophie, a one-legged pirate called Pierre, a ruffian called Jean, a squeaky rat called Isabelle and a goat called Chou-Chou who likes to eat cabbages! They all have very distinct personalities, which are conveyed through their body language and my tone of voice.

There is no need to have any skill in ventriloquism, the children will quite happily interact with the puppet and respond to 'its' questions as though you were not there. Interestingly, sometimes the 'shy' puppet Sophie whispers (inaudibly) an answer to a question in a child's ear. When I enquire what the response was, the child always knows!

Soft toys

Soft toys are particularly appropriate when introducing vocabulary for animals but can also be used in other games. They can easily be acquired at jumble sales, car boot sales or by asking for donations. To get the most out of them linguistically, choose ones which are different colours and sizes, and which appear to have different characters, as well as those representing common household pets.

Oracy
O3.3, O4.4, O5.1, O5.2, O6.2

The following activities allow for practice of conversations including asking and answering questions and expressing opinions, as well as using puppets for performance. In addition, the activities using soft toys allow vocabulary to be recalled and used, and encourage children to listen attentively.

Practising language using single words or short phrases, asking and answering questions

31. Model puppets

✦ When practising asking and answering questions, use one of your puppets! Ask a child to come to the front of the class to ask the puppet questions such as 'What is your name?', 'Do you like the colour blue?' or 'Do you have any pets?'

✦ Your puppet then responds and asks the child the same question.

✦ Once several children have come to the front of the class to ask and answer questions, this will have provided the rest of the class with a good linguistic model which they can use as they ask and answer questions with one another.

✦ Alternatively, when they come to the front of the class, they can get their puppets to ask and answer the questions, making it more interesting as no-one knows what the puppets will 'say'.

32. **Puppet fun**

✦ If you arrange for a day when everyone brings in a puppet from home, whether homemade or commercially produced, a fun lesson can ensue.

✦ There will be a real buzz and excitement in the air as the children circulate with their puppets, interacting with each other's puppets to ask questions and seek information.

33. **Puppet mind-reading**

✦ Ask a child to stand up with his/her puppet and to ask it to 'think' of a word, statement or opinion.

✦ Then say that the other children or puppets need to try to find out what it is by asking questions. This could be a class, group or pair activity.

34. **Reveal the pet**

✦ Place a number of soft toy animals in a large box or bag.

✦ Slowly reveal an animal showing only the tip of an ear, tail or paw at first.

✦ The first child to recognize the toy and state the name of the animal gets to hold it.

35. **Pass the animal**

✦ This is always a popular and frenetic game. Ask a child to state which pet s/he owns or would like. The appropriate soft toy is handed over.

✦ Once all the soft toys are distributed, tell the children that if they want to hold any of the soft toys in the room, all they have to do is ask for it in the appropriate way.

✦ Allow one person to ask at a time but move quickly on to the next person, whilst the toy is being handed over. This means it is a quick fire activity.

✦ Not only does this activity give the children practice in using the language but it requires them to listen attentively as well. The game also ensures that the soft toys pass through as many hands as possible.

36. **Hunt the bear**

✦ The game 'hunt the thimble' works very well if instead of a thimble a soft toy is used.

✦ Choose a child to go out of the room, and ask another child to hide a soft toy somewhere in the room, ideally with a little part of it showing.

✦ Invite the first child to come back in. The rest of the class then guides the child to it by saying a sequence of words, loudly as the child gets near and softly when the child is far away.

✦ This is a game which is popular and frequently requested. I use a small brown bear called Mimi which has found itself hidden in all kinds of places!

37. **Hands under the table**

✦ I use Mimi in this popular game too (see activity 36). Of course, any soft toy will do.

✦ Choose a child to go out of the room.

✦ Give the soft toy to a child in the room. Tell everyone to put their hands under the desk including the person who has the soft toy.

✦ The first child re-enters the classroom and practises asking a particular question to one child at a time.

✦ Each child responds in an appropriate way in the target language except for the child with the soft toy who calls out 'Mimi!', or whatever the name of the soft toy is.

✦ If two or three children are involved in asking the question, it becomes a race. Great fun!

38. **Puppet story-telling**

✦ Puppets give older children an opportunity to retell a story or rhyme which they have been reading in class. This could be, for example, a familiar fairy tale recounted in the target language.

✦ Appropriately dressed puppets could be used to act it out and retell it.

✦ You could ask older children in Key Stage 2 to perform the story or rhyme to the younger children or parents in a class assembly.

Literacy

Puppets and soft toys are generally better suited to practising oracy than literacy skills. However, the following idea is useful.

Writing simple words or phrases using a model

39. Puppet display

✦ Once the children have brought puppets to school and practised oracy skills, if they don't mind being parted from them for a while, pin them to a display board in the classroom.

✦ Then ask the children to write in a paper speech bubble what they are saying, such as their name or an opinion.

✦ The puppets are then available for reviews of learning as necessary and are at hand when next needed to perform.

Realia

The tactile or kinaesthetic style of learning is dominant among primary age children. Being able to hold an object about which you are talking not only reinforces the learning but also appears to make it more enjoyable. Most of the objects mentioned below can usually be found somewhere in a Key Stage 1 or 2 classroom. Any language specific items which are not so easily sourced can be made. It can be a little time-consuming but it is definitely cheaper than buying commercially made products.

For example, baguettes, croissants and ice cream cones preserved with a non-aqueous based varnish last for years. With a little imagination, other items can be made. I use cotton wool dipped in food colouring for scoops of ice cream. I have collected items of clothing from jumble sales. I save packets and bottles from the countries where the target language is spoken. Not only can these items be used in class for practising language but they can also make up a display.

Many of the activities described in the 'Flashcards' section can be used with realia instead of cards.

Year 6 children role-playing being in a café

Oracy   O3.1, O3.2, O3.3, O3.4, O4.2, O4.3, O4.4, O5.1, O6.2

Rhymes, stories and songs inevitably entail some kind of story-telling. The 'story' can be made to come alive by using realia. Using realia in the activities described in this chapter also encourages children to listen attentively, be aware of specific sounds and recall vocabulary.

Realia is also a must when children are performing and practising longer conversations and role-plays. They make the situations seem more real and provide a natural stimulus to which they have to respond.

Oral communication is a performance. By giving the children the opportunity to perform their conversation or role-play to the rest of the class or a larger audience, the performance is taken one step further than a simple interaction in pairs. It is communication for a purpose. It is worthwhile considering asking the children to lead an assembly or put on a show in the target language, so as to be able to 'perform' to the rest of the school and parents.

Responding to rhymes, stories and songs

40. Props in songs

✦ The meaning of a story, song or rhyme can be reinforced if props are used.

✦ Select children to hold, wear or move the appropriate props as they are recited.

✦ For example with year 4 classes, I sing a version of 'The farmer's in his den' in the target language. The children are always desperate to be the one to wear the battered old straw hat to be the farmer, the headscarf to be the wife, and so on.

✦ I sing a song with a year 6 class about a restaurant where all the items are 'off' the menu. This is a linguistically challenging song. However, by using props such as a menu, table and tablecloth, it makes it more accessible and understandable.

✦ The only challenge, I sometimes find, is making sure that the children do not become so engrossed with the props and the acting that they forget to sing!

Listening for specific words, sounds and rhyme

41. **Build a pile**

✦ Provide the children with piles of plastic linking bricks.

✦ Ask them to add a brick to the pile every time they hear a certain word or phrase.

✦ Check at the end to see how many bricks each child has.

42. **Which colour?**

✦ This activity is a variation on activity 41 and encourages the children to listen attentively.

✦ Provide each child or group of children with a selection of coloured bricks.

✦ Say colours aloud in a specific order and ask the children to build a tower with the bricks in that same order.

43. **Sort by category**

✦ Provide a selection of objects. Say aloud the word for one of these objects.

✦ Ask the children to listen carefully and select the correct object, then sort it into an appropriate pile according to a particular sound or syllables.

✦ As you probably won't have enough objects for the whole class to use at the same time, select individuals to come out and sort them.

44. **Pick and show**

✦ As a variation on activity 43, give several groups of children a selection of items representing different vocabulary.

✦ Read out the name of each item, and ask a member of each group to raise the appropriate object in the air when they hear its name.

✦ This could be a competitive game between teams to see who is the first to select and show.

✦ If you do not have enough items for several groups, split the class into two teams and provide two piles of items. Ask for representatives from each team to compete against each other.

45. Dressing up

✦　If you are practising the words for clothes, try this fun game with willing children.

✦　Provide two piles of clothes identical in type and colour.

✦　Name an item of clothing and its colour.

✦　A point goes to the team who correctly identifies and puts on the item of clothing first. This is guaranteed to have the children in fits of laughter.

Practising language using single words or phrases

46. **Please and thank you**

✦ This is an extremely simple game to practise the words for 'please' and 'thank you'.

✦ Give a child an object, such as a ball.

✦ The child sitting next to him/her asks for the object politely, the child with the object hands it over and the child receiving it thanks him/her. For example, one child says 'I would like the ball, please,' and the child with the ball passes it and says 'Here you are.' The other child takes the ball and says 'Thank you.' This continues around the class or circle.

✦ To allow for the greatest amount of child participation, provide several objects which can be passed around at the same time.

47. **Feel in the bag**

'Feely bags' mean secrecy and surprise, two 'key ingredients' for ensuring a positive response from children. A feely bag can be any kind of bag, such as a homemade drawstring bag, a P.E. bag, a carrier bag or even a cardboard box with a hole.

Place objects representing the vocabulary which the children have been learning in the feely bag.

Ask a child to feel for an object and say what it is before taking it out.

Once removed from the bag, ask the rest of the class for confirmation of the correct word or phrase given. If it is correct, the item is retained by the child, if not, it is returned to the bag.

48. **Yes or no?**

✦ This activity is particularly useful for practising adjectives and works well as a team game.

Present to the class similar objects in a variety of colours, sizes or shapes, such as pencils of different colours.

Place one object in a feely bag (see activity 47) without the class seeing what it is.

✦ Ask the children to guess what the object is by making statements like 'It's a small blue pencil.' You reply by saying either 'yes' or 'no'.

If the answer is 'no', another child makes a guess.

✦ If the answer is 'yes', it is that child's turn to put something in the feely bag for the others to guess.

Asking and answering questions

49. **What's in the bag?**

✦ Place a familiar object, e.g. a soft toy animal to practise pet vocabulary, in a feely bag (see activity 47), without letting the children see it.

✦ Allow the children a certain number of questions to guess what it is. The type of questions will depend on the ability of the group. Simple questions might include 'Is it big?' or 'Is it brown?', and more complex ones could be 'Does it have two long ears?' or 'Does it swim in the sea?'

✦ You can only reply 'yes' or 'no' to their questions.

50. **Pardon?**

✦ Distribute a variety of well-known objects amongst the children.

✦ Each child tells the child next to him/her what the object is.

✦ The second child should pretend not to understand what has been said and say 'Pardon? What is it?' in the target language.

✦ The first child repeats what s/he said and the second child now feigns understanding and repeats the word or phrase.

✦ This process continues around the room.

*Preparing, practising and performing simple
conversations and role-plays*

51. **On the phone**

✦ Try using two telephones and ask the children to sit back-to-back whilst holding a conversation. This makes the interaction more challenging, as there are no visual clues.

✦ This is a particularly authentic setting for discussing the weather as normally you would never ask someone what the weather is like if you are in the same place.

52. **Buying and selling**

✦ Using realia in conversations related to buying and selling means that the element of choice is introduced which renders the communication more authentic. For example, there could be a choice of colour, size or style, or there simply may not be any of that particular item.

53. **Creative role-playing**

✦ Conversations and role-plays provide great scope for children to be creative, and it is amazing how many different ways children can think of to use a dialogue which might have quite limited language content.

✦ Ask the children to select a different personality, mood, profession, venue and what they are doing each time they act out a dialogue, and before they start to practise the language.

✦ For example, a simple exchange of information between two people about their names, ages and how they are feeling could be acted out as if they are:
  - Two friends in the park whilst playing football
  - Two people in the disco who can't hear each other very well due to the loud music and have to shout
  - A policeman and a child who is lost, in the street
  - Two children at school, where one is trying to make friends with the other, who is shy

✦ The possibilities are endless and they make for more interesting listening when you ask the children to demonstrate and share their dialogues with the rest of the class.

Literacy

The following are ways in which the realia could be used to practise writing using a model or as a starting point for writing.

Writing simple words and phrases using a model

54. Writing labels

✦ Use realia to make a classroom display and ask the children to write labels for the objects.

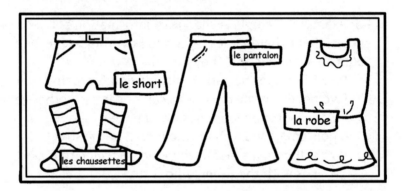

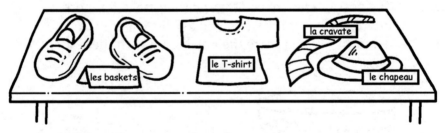

55. Favourite foods

✦ If real foods have been brought into the classroom for children to try, the packaging could be saved and displayed.

✦ Carry out a survey to find out which foods each child likes.

✦ Ask the children to write down what they think about different foods and display the writing with the packets.

Balls, beanbags and dice

Balls, beanbags and dice involve several of the 'key ingredients', namely manipulation, physical movement and surprise. For some children, a ball, beanbag or large soft die is an unexpected resource and it captures their interest. There are potential hazards in using them in the classroom; accuracy of shot and coordination are not always well developed in primary children. However, reminders and a demonstration of how to pass them usually avoid most problems. Alternatively, these activities could take place in the school hall or playground.

Any small, soft, spongy ball is suitable; I find stress-relief balls particularly apt. Beanbags can be found in most primary school resource cupboards.

Year 5 children playing 'Pass and answer'

Balls, beanbags and dice

As well as using traditional six-sided dice for board games and number work, it is possible to purchase blank dice and large sponge dice. The six sides provide opportunities to practise vocabulary and phrases in a random and unpredictable way. By applying stickers to its sides, with appropriate images, colours, numbers, etc. you can customize a blank die. To each side of a large sponge die, I attach one part of self-adhesive hoop and loop fastener and attach the other part to an image (preferably laminated). The images on each side of the die can be easily changed thus making it a versatile resource for different topics.

Oracy

O3.2, O3.3, O3.4, O4.4

These games with balls, bean bags and dice encourage children to listen for particular sounds, words and phrases, as well as to respond to them, perform simple communicative tasks and respond to questions.

Practising language using single words or phrases

56. **Add up the dice**

✦ If your school's resource cupboard has enough dice to give small teams of children two or three dice each, you could play a simple elimination game.

✦ Ask the children to roll the dice and add up the numbers.

✦ Each team tells the rest what their total is and the team with the lowest number goes out. The game continues until only one group remains.

57. **Snakes and ladders**

It is possible to create a simple board game using a grid of squares.

To practise numbers in the target language, number each square in sequence and, if possible, superimpose snakes and ladders over the grid. This will create a traditional 'snakes and ladders' game.

Organize the class into small groups of about four children and provide them with a grid, counters and a die.

Ask the children to take turns at throwing the die and saying aloud the number, then counting forward that number of squares in the target language. Obviously, landing on a square with a ladder means that they move to the top of the ladder and landing on a snake means they must descend to the tail of the snake.

Hint: To ensure that the target language is used as the counter is moved forward, insist on the rule that if the number is said in English, the player must go back that number of squares. The children always take this very seriously.

58. **Throw and say**

As an alternative to numbers on a snakes and ladders board (activity 57), images could be added to some or all of the squares so that every time the children land on an image, they have to say the word or create a sentence using that word.

If they are unable to do this, they should miss a go.

59. **Secret die**

✦ This involves the 'key ingredient' of trying to discover a secret, making it a popular game.

✦ Customize a blank die or a large soft die by attaching images such as classroom objects or colours.

✦ Find a box large enough so that the die can be thrown inside it but remain hidden from view. Empty photocopy paper boxes are ideal and often easily accessible.

✦ Ask a child in each group to throw the die inside the box.

✦ The task for the other children is to find out which image is showing upwards. Each child in the group should be allowed one turn at a time to guess what it is (using phrases such as 'It is blue' if you are using colour flashcards attached to the die).

✦ The first person to discover what the image is, swaps with the thrower and the game starts again.

✦ Keep a tally or use counters, to see who was the most successful.

60. **Throw and mime**

✦ As a variation on activity 59, you could attach images of hobbies or classroom commands to the die.

✦ Ask the children to throw the die in the box, then mime the activity. The other children should be encouraged to guess in the target language what the activity is.

✦ Alternatively you could ask the child to give an instruction to the rest of the class to do a particular action according to the image on the die.

✦ Using images of famous personalities or cartoon characters always causes great hilarity especially if you include characters considered to be too young for their 'mature' years.

✦ Once again ask the children to throw the sponge die and then act out the character on the die so that the others have to guess who it is.

✦ For more able children, there is an opportunity here to practise asking questions.

Asking and answering questions

61. **Pass and answer**

✦ It never ceases to amaze me how being able to catch and pass a ball or beanbag is so motivating. Everyone seems to want to do it.

✦ Balls and beanbags can be used to review questions and answers previously practised. This works well at the start of a lesson.

✦ The child with the ball or beanbag says the name of another child, asks a question, and then throws it to that person. The child receiving the ball or beanbag answers the question appropriately.

✦ Hint: Encouraging the throwers to name the child they are addressing so s/he knows the ball or beanbag is coming is a good idea, because otherwise the ball or beanbag spends a lot of time on the floor!

62. Lip-reading

✦ For variety, instead of saying a question aloud and then passing the ball or beanbag (activity 61), try mouthing it silently instead.

✦ It requires more concentration and focuses the children on mouth shape formation, which helps with pronunciation.

63. Balls everywhere

✦ In order to give as many children as possible an opportunity to practise at one time, divide the class into groups and repeat activities 61 or 62 using several balls or beanbags.

✦ Forfeits, such as 'stand on one leg', 'use one arm', etc. could be given to anyone who drops the ball or beanbag or can't answer the questions.

64. **Musical ball**

✦ If you would prefer the children not to throw the ball or beanbag, try playing some music in the target language as the children pass it around the group (see activity 61).

✦ The child holding the ball or beanbag when the music stops, asks the person of his/her choice a question.

Listening for specific words and phrases

65. Grab the beanbag

✦   This is a good game for the hall or playground.

✦   Divide the class into two equal teams.

✦   Assign a different number, item of vocabulary or phrase to every child on one team.

✦   Use the same numbers or items to name every child on the opposing team, so you end up with each number or item assigned to one child per team.

✦   Line up the two teams facing each other, about five or six metres apart. Use lines marked on the ground, if possible, as this helps to keep the teams equidistant.

✦　Place a beanbag on the ground halfway between the two teams.

✦　Call out an item or number, or show a corresponding flashcard, and the child from each team who is responsible for that word or phrase rushes to pick up the beanbag first and get back to his/her place in the line before being caught by the other child. This earns one point for that team.

✦　Hint: If both children arrive at the beanbag at the same time, tell them that it is best to wait before they seize it as the one with the bag will immediately be caught. Tell them to grab the beanbag after a slight pause when they think the other child won't be expecting it.

Literacy

This is quite a challenging game which gives children practice in constructing familiar phrases.

Reading, recognizing and understanding familiar words in written form

66. Roll and construct a sentence

✦ Write a familiar sentence on card and cut it up into six pieces with individual words or phrases on each. Randomly number the pieces from one to six.

✦ In small groups, ask the children to roll a die in order to collect the necessary pieces to reconstruct the sentence.

✦ To make it even more challenging, you could ask the children to collect the pieces in the correct order or numbered superfluous words could also be given.

✦ Hint: A card with the correct order of words would be useful with which the children could check their sentence at the end.

Get up and move

Getting up and moving involves yet another of the 'key ingredients' to which I referred in the introduction. Channelling the abundance of energy in a Key Stage 2 child into effective learning is rewarding.

Small classrooms crammed with children, desks, chairs, trays, books, boxes, computers, etc. are not always an ideal environment for these activities. Consideration of the health and safety issues is needed. Nevertheless many of these activities are possible within the confines of a classroom. Moving beyond the classroom to the hall or playground is an even better solution.

Year 4 children playing 'Human sequence' with the days of the week

Oracy

O3.2, O3.3, O3.4, O4.3, O4.4, O5.2

These games require some kind of physical response, or practise language while moving. The games towards the end of this section allow the children to practise asking and answering questions as well as specifically finding out likes and dislikes.

Listening, recognizing and responding to sounds and words

67. Stand up, sit down

✦ First of all, divide the class into groups; if they are sitting around tables, this is easy to organize.

✦ Give each group a word or phrase. Tell them that when they hear the word or sound, they should stand up together.

✦ Call out the words or phrases. If you vary the pace of this activity, you will find that the faster you go, the more it is appreciated.

✦ For a change, sometimes I say the words or phrases in English, and the children stand up and respond in the target language.

68. Simon says

✦ One of the most popular of all physical response games is 'Simon says'. I change the name 'Simon' for an appropriate name in the target language.

✦ This is one of my most requested games. It works particularly well with classroom actions but can also be used for any topic to which the children can produce a physical response, for example, hobbies, or any sentences using a variety of verbs.

✦ I'm sure you know the game but in case you don't, if you ask the children to do an action and you say 'Simon says', they do it.

✦ A request without 'Simon says' means that they continue to do the last action.

✦ If they start to do the action when Simon doesn't say so, they are out.

✦ This is one of the most challenging games to bring to a conclusion and find a winner. The children become so proficient at it, especially in years 5 and 6, it is hard to catch them out. Try using children already eliminated to spot anyone making an error or ask the remaining few to stand at the front in clear view of everyone.

✦ It is great fun and I'm sure you will be asked to play it again and again.

69. **Don't do it!**

✦ Try activity 68 but this time use negative commands, so not only must the children not do the action if Simon says not to, but they must also do the action if you say not to without saying 'Simon says'.

✦ Very confusing and very challenging – for both the teacher and the children!

70. **Quick draw**

✦ Divide the class into two teams and ask for a representative from each team to stand at the board.

✦ Say a word or phrase and the first person to draw an appropriate image on the board wins a point.

✦ This also works well with numbers.

71. **Odds and evens**

✦ This is another game for practising numbers.

✦ Ask the children to stand up.

✦ Tell them that when they hear an even number they should rub their stomach, and when they hear an odd number they should pat their head. (It is not important what the actions are, you can choose whatever you like.)

✦ Any child caught doing the wrong action at the wrong time is out.

✦ This activity reinforces mathematical knowledge as well as linguistic skills.

72. **Fruit salad**

✦ The children need to be sitting on chairs in a circle.

✦ Give every child a word or phrase to remember, with each word allocated to more than one child.

✦ Call out one of these and everyone responsible for it must get up and find a new seat.

✦ Occasionally, call out 'Fruit Salad' and everyone must change places.

✦ You could ask a child to stand in the centre of the circle and call out the words instead of you. This child should then try to take the place of one of the children who gets up. It is then the turn of this child to call out the words or phrases.

73. **Grab the card**

✦ You need a lot of room to play this game.

✦ Divide the class into two teams and number the children in each team.

✦ Place flashcards around the room, then call out a number and name an object on one of the cards.

✦ The first child with the corresponding number who brings the flashcard to you wins a point.

74. **Catch me if you can**

✦ This game needs to be played in an open space.

✦ Arrange the children in a line.

✦ Using two words or phrases, give the first to the first child, the second to the second, the first to the third, and so on, alternately.

✦ Call out one of the words or phrases and the children who have ownership of it, have to try to touch an agreed point, such as a wall, before the other children catch them.

✦ Once caught they are out until only one child remains.

75. **Left, right, straight on**

✦ This is a particularly good game for practising directions.

✦ Ask a child to stand up and move away from his/her seat.

✦ Blindfold the child. (Hint: Try using the blindfolds given out on aeroplanes to block out the light and help you sleep.)

✦ Then ask another child to direct the blindfolded child back to his/her seat. Each command, left or right, means the child should turn 90 degrees in that direction. Don't forget to teach the word 'stop'.

✦ To ensure safety, remember to monitor the blindfolded person, removing any obstacles out of the way.

76. **Twister®**

✦   If you can get hold of several boxes of the Twister® game, you can play it in the target language. This will obviously give the children practice in recognizing the words for parts of the body, left and right, as well as colours.

✦   Either one child in each group can spin the dial and call out the instructions, or you can spin one dial for all the groups at the same time.

✦   Be prepared – this is a very noisy activity when thirty or more children are involved at the same time. You could make table versions of the mat and the children could use their fingers – this is not as much fun though and rather fiddly.

77. **Stand up and say**

✦ This activity adds a competitive element to the 'stand up, sit down' game (activity 67) and gives the children an opportunity to practise the language item for their group.

✦ Give each group a word or phrase and tell them that when they hear their word or phrase the first person in that group to stand up and repeat it wins a point.

✦ Call out the words or phrases and award points to the children who stand up and repeat their group's language item first.

✦ Children seem to really like this game.

78. **Higher or lower**

✦ Many children love the idea of being able to leave their seat and come to the front of the class. There is never a shortage of volunteers even before they know what they will be doing!

✦ This game allows them to practise their mathematical skills as well as linguistic ones.

✦ One child comes to the front of the class and thinks of a number, for example, between one and twenty.

✦ Another child makes a guess as to what it might be, and the child who has thought of the number says whether it is higher, lower or correct.

✦ The child who guesses correctly has the next turn of thinking of a number.

79. What am I thinking of?

✦ Another even simpler form of activity 78 is to ask a child to come to the front and think of an item of vocabulary and then allow the other children a certain number of guesses to find out what it is.

80. Eleven

✦ I have never really understood why this game is so popular, but be assured it will be among the most requested games. I have taught some classes who want to play it every single lesson.

✦ It is based on the numbers one to eleven, although any eleven numbers in sequence could be used.

✦ Ask the children to stand up. Choose a child to start, who says one, two or three numbers in sequence starting at number one.

✦ The next child follows in the same way, carrying on from the last number saying either one, two or three numbers.

✦ In order to stay in the game, you must not be the person who says number eleven. The child who is forced to say eleven because the person before him/her has said ten is out and must sit down.

✦ The number sequence restarts at number one and the game continues until only one person remains, who is the winner.

81. **Secret signal**

✦ Write up a list of words or phrases on the board in the target language.

✦ Ask one child to leave the room and agree with the rest of the class on a secret signal, such as scratching the side of one's nose.

✦ Choose a child to perform this signal at any given moment.

✦ Bring the first child back into the room and ask the class to say over and over again the first item from the list on the board.

✦ Every time the class sees the designated person do the agreed secret signal, they move on to the next word or phrase in the list.

✦ The idea of the game is to see if the person who went outside can work out who is doing the secret signal which changes the word each time.

✦ Of course, meanwhile, the children are given a lot of opportunity to repeat and practise the words or phrases.

82. **Mime**

✦ Some children love to mime and perform in front of the rest of the class – this activity appeals to them.

✦ Ask for a volunteer to mime an action.

✦ Tell the children that when they know what it is, they should say it in the target language.

83. **Hello, goodbye**

✦ This is a very simple but popular game to practise saying hello and goodbye.

✦ Ask the children to stand in a circle facing inwards.

✦ One child walks around the outside of the circle in a clockwise direction, tapping each child on the shoulder and saying hello in the target language.

✦ When the child taps the shoulder of a child and says goodbye, both of them run clockwise around the circle to see who can be the first to get back to the empty place in the circle.

✦ Whichever of them is last is the person who then walks around the edge of the circle saying hello.

84. **Chinese whispers**

✦ Form the class into teams of about eight, standing in lines.

✦ Give a word or phrase to the first child in each team, which s/he must whisper in the next person's ear.

✦ The second child then whispers the word or phrase to the next child, and so on along the line.

✦ When the message reaches the last person in the line, s/he should then either rush to you to say what it is, select an appropriate flashcard, or write it on the board.

✦ It is not necessary to give the same word or phrase to each group.

85. **Draw with a finger**

✦ This game works well with numbers.

✦ Ask the children to find a partner each.

✦ One child in each pair thinks of a number and draws it with his/her finger on the other child's back.

✦ The other child must say what s/he thinks it is in the target language.

✦ If the answer is correct, they swap roles.

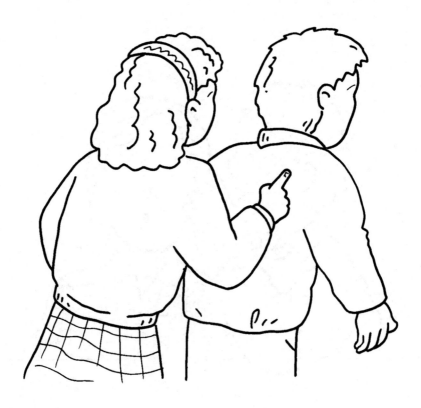

86. Mexican wave

✦ Performing a Mexican wave is usually popular.

✦ Choose a list of vocabulary; words often learnt in sequence are best for this, such as numbers, days and months.

✦ Decide on the sequence around the room, namely who goes first, second, etc.

✦ Ask the children to stand up in turn, throw their arms in the air and say the next item on the list. As soon as one child has sat down, the next child should perform his/her word and so on until the last person is reached.

✦ I often time them doing this with a stopwatch and then they have several tries to improve their time.

87. **Picture dictation**

✦ Form two or three teams and secretly show the same picture to one member of each team.

✦ Each team member returns to the rest of the team and draws the image.

✦ The first team to say in the target language what is being drawn wins a point.

✦ Hint: It is better not to have too many teams so as to be able to hear who says the word or phrase first.

Asking and answering questions

88. Circles

✦ Form two circles of an equal number of children, with one circle inside the other. Ask the outside circle to face inwards and the inside circle to face outwards.

✦ Call out a number in the target language.

✦ The outside circle should move in a clockwise direction that number of paces so that they are now facing a different person.

✦ The person in the outside circle asks the person in the inside circle a question, who responds appropriately.

✦ It may take a few practices to get one circle to move in the correct direction and the other circle to stand still.

✦ For variety, ask the inner circle to move, change the direction of movement, or ask the children on the inside to ask those on the outside a question.

89. **What's the time, Mr Wolf?**

✦ The principle of the traditional game 'What's the time, Mr Wolf?' can be used to practise questions and answers for any topic, not just time.

✦ The 'wolf' stands at the front with his/her back to everyone else, and the rest of the group asks a pre-determined question.

✦ The wolf cannot turn around until s/he has answered the question, during which time the rest of the children try to move forward as close to the wolf as possible.

✦ After answering the question the wolf spins around. If s/he spots the other children moving, these have to go back to the start. If the wolf does not see them move, they start from where they are for the next question.

✦ The winner is the first person to touch the wolf on the back without being seen.

✦ Rather than use the same question every time, to make it more challenging, you can hold up prompt cards which the wolf can't see.

✦ This is obviously a game best played in the hall or playground.

90. Find Mr X

✦ Although I call this game 'Find Mr X', of course it could be 'Mrs X' or even 'Miss X'!

✦ Give each child a square of paper. Most of the pieces of paper should be blank but three or four pieces should have a cross on them. (Hint: Make sure the paper is thick enough for the cross not to be seen through it.)

✦ The children circulate in the room, practising a question and answer on the current topic. However, the children who are 'Mr X' can only respond with 'My name is Mr X.'

✦ When the children ask the question and receive the response 'My name is Mr X,' they should sit down quietly without telling anyone else who Mr X is. Otherwise they continue to circulate asking other children the question.

✦ The game continues until only the Mr Xs remain.

✦ You will find that everyone wants to be Mr X. This game has the 'key ingredient' of the shared secret, which is probably why it is so popular.

91. **Find your partner**

✦ Give each child a piece of paper with some information on it such as a name or age. Each piece of information should appear on two pieces of paper.

✦ The idea of the game is to find the person with the same information as you by asking and responding to questions. For example, use this to practise asking for and saying a name; it works particularly well if you use the names of famous people or characters.

✦ Once a pair have found each other, they both sit down.

✦ When all the children have found their partner, ask them to tell the class who they are – this always provokes much hilarity.

✦ This activity ensures a lot of practice in answering and asking questions as well as social interaction.

92. **Find your group**

✦ Activity 91 works well if several children have the same information.

✦ Once one child has found someone with the same word or phrase, they stay together and find someone else to add to their group.

✦ The children seem to love discovering who is in their group and having a sense of belonging to it.

✦ The game continues until all the children are in a group.

✦ Then ask each group the relevant question and they reply in unison.

93. **Find someone who...**

✦ To practise likes and dislikes, choose a suitable topic using vocabulary which the children already know, such as food.

✦ Give each child two grids of images for this topic, one under a symbol for 'like' and the other under a symbol for 'dislike'.

✦ Ask the children to interview others in the class to find a different person for a variety of categories, for example, someone who likes chocolate, someone who doesn't like cabbage, etc. The child writes the name of the person under the relevant image.

✦ Once completed, ask the class to share their findings.

94. Cock-a-doodle-do

✦ This game involves a child leaving the room and being excluded, and then discovering a shared secret, an assured ingredient in the recipe for success.

✦ When the child is out of the room, choose two or three children to respond with a special phrase when they are asked a question. In fact, I often ask the whole class to respond with this phrase when one of these children is asked a question. I use the words for 'cock-a-doodle-do' in the target language, but you could use any phrase.

✦ Tell all the other children to respond with an appropriate answer when they are asked a question.

✦ The child who has left the room returns and asks children of his/her choice a question, until s/he hears the special phrase.

✦ I find that children are as desperate to be the person to discover the secret as they are to be one of those who say 'cock-a-doodle-do'.

95. Question chain

✦ Form teams of about six children and ask them to stand in a line.

✦ Ask the first child to turn to the second child and ask a question, to which the second child responds.

✦ This questioning and answering continues down the line until the last child gives an answer.

✦ To make this competitive, I usually time how long it takes for each team to finish.

✦ There is a tendency for the question and answer to become a little mangled and difficult to discern, so insist on clarity.

✦ To make this really challenging, you could suggest that each child asks a different question.

96. **Mastermind**

✦ The class arranges itself into teams and names its team.

✦ Representatives from each team take it in turns to take the 'hot seat' and compete against the other representatives to be the first to answer a question correctly.

✦ I use a bell, such as you find on hotel reception desks, and it is the first person to ring the bell and answer the question correctly who wins the point.

✦ This is a good game to play as a means of reviewing a topic or series of topics.

97. **Who is speaking?**

✦ Ask a child to come to the front of the class and stand with his/her back to the other children.

✦ This child asks a question and someone in the room replies trying to disguise his/her voice.

✦ The child at the front has to guess who it is.

✦ Hint: To avoid more than one child speaking at a time, you could point to a child to answer the question.

Literacy

L3.1, L3.3, L4.1, L4.3, L4.4, L5.2, L5.3

These activities involve reading and/or writing.

Reading, recognizing and understanding familiar words and phrases in written form

98. Human sequence

◆ This is a reading activity that works particularly well with vocabulary which is often learnt in sequence, such as numbers or the days of the week.

◆ Ask the same number of children as there are items of vocabulary to line up.

◆ Give each child a card face down, with a different item of vocabulary on it.

◆ Then ask the children to turn over the cards and arrange themselves from left to right across the room so that the cards are in sequence.

◆ This involves the children reading not only their card but also those of the others in their group.

◆ I sometimes use a stopwatch to time how long it takes for the children to line up correctly.

99. **Human sentence**

◆ This is like activity 98, but for children with more advanced reading skills.

◆ Give them cards with individual words and ask them to rearrange them in an appropriate way to form a sentence.

◆ Timing it makes it more challenging and groups can compete against each other.

100. Hangman

✦ This old favourite is still a very popular game.

✦ One child thinks of a word and indicates how many letters there are in this word by drawing the appropriate number of dashes.

✦ The rest of the class guesses the letters, but an incorrect guess means another section of the hangman is drawn.

✦ If the child manages to complete the hangman before the word is guessed, s/he wins.

101. **Write with a finger**

✦ In activity 85 I described how children can trace a number on their partner's back.

✦ Try the same activity but this time ask the children to trace letters to write a familiar word which their partner must guess in the target language.

✦ If the guess is correct they swap roles.

102. Running dictation

♦ Pin copies of the same list of familiar words or phrases around the room. These need to be far enough away from the children so that they cannot be read without them leaving their seats.

♦ Ask the children to find a partner or form a small group, and allocate a list to each group.

♦ One child from each group has to go and read the list and then return to his/her partner or group and say it aloud. Ask the receiving group to write down what is being said (the runner is not allowed to write anything down).

♦ If the list is quite long, it will require the runner to go backwards and forwards between the paper and the group.

♦ This activity works well with a shopping list or ingredients for a recipe.

♦ Decide on the level of accuracy expected.

♦ The first group to finish is the winner.

103. **Treasure hunt**

✦ Organize a simple treasure hunt around the school using written clues which the children follow to find the treasure.

✦ Depending on the ability of the children, you could ask them to write their own clues, perhaps using a dictionary. They could then swap their clues with another group.

✦ Each group should have a different hiding place and their own 'treasure'.

104. **Scavenger hunt**

✦ This is a little easier to organize than a treasure hunt.

✦ Give the children a list of items to be found, for example, a brown leaf, something red, three stones, all written in the target language, of course.

✦ The winners are the first group to come back with all these items.

✦ You could ask the children to devise their own list for others to use.

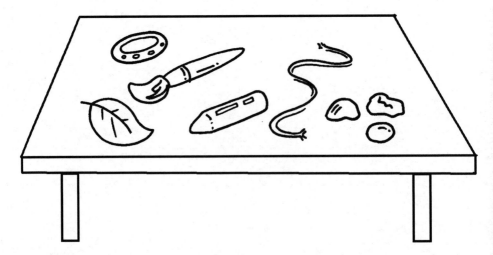

Interactive whiteboard

The interactive whiteboard is a very versatile resource which can be used in numerous ways in teaching and practising a language. Flashcards and the use of an ordinary board can be substituted by an interactive whiteboard for many of the activities described in other chapters.

The advantage of using the interactive whiteboard is that these activities can be saved and accessed easily for future use. This alleviates the problem of storage of bulky materials in paper form and makes it easier for staff in a school to share materials. In addition, using an interactive whiteboard is also a cheaper way of producing and presenting the materials. Colour can be used without the worry of expensive copying costs and images are easy to find.

Year 5 children playing 'Noughts and crosses'

Interactive whiteboard

The following activities are ones which require the use of the interactive facility of the board rather than just projection mode. For the same reasons that children enjoy kinaesthetic activities, most children love to manipulate and move images on an interactive whiteboard.

It is possible to find internet sites providing interactive exercises to use in the classroom, for free. In addition, there are sites to which you can pay an annual subscription which have a wide array of fun games on a variety of topics. However, with a basic understanding of Microsoft Word software and/or the whiteboard software, it is possible to create your own interactive exercises. Hint: Always use landscape rather than portrait format so there is no need to move the image up and down to view it all. Creating and customizing your own exercises leaves you free to choose the language content and structure which is appropriate for your class.

Oracy

Many of the activities below rely on some kind of 'click-and-drag box' to conceal words or images. Creating these activities can be time-consuming but once the initial format is constructed, the images and words can be substituted by others for different topics. The documents could be placed on the school network or website to give children an opportunity for further practice through independent work.

Practising language using single words or phrases

105. **What is it?**

✦   Produce a document with images which represent the vocabulary currently being learnt.

✦   Create some 'click-and-drag' boxes the same size as the images so that they can be concealed.

✦   Slowly reveal the image by clicking and dragging the box and ask the children to guess what it is.

✦   If your whiteboard software has a 'spotlight' function which allows you to present a small part of the board at one time, this would work just as well.

106. **Noughts and crosses**

✦ Produce a grid of three squares by three squares and into each square insert an image or number.

✦ Prepare at least ten 'click-and-drag' boxes which are the same size as the squares and superimpose either O or X on each.

✦ Divide the class into two teams and name them O or X.

✦ Each team takes a turn. If a member of the team can correctly produce the item of language for a given square, cover that square with O or X.

✦ The winning team is the one which achieves three Os or three Xs in a row.

107. **Find the sweets**

✦ Produce 'click-and-drag' boxes with images superimposed on them.

✦ Behind one of these boxes hide an image of a well-known character, sweets, a pot of gold, etc.

✦ Ask a child to name one of the images, move this aside and see if it reveals the sought after item.

✦ If it does, ask the class to close their eyes while the child jumbles up the images and conceals the special image with a different box.

✦ This child can then choose a child to name a box and reveal if it is the correct one or not.

108. Kim's game

◆   This game does not involve 'click-and-drag' boxes but the application 'Powerpoint'.

◆   It is possible to create a version of 'Kim's game' for the interactive whiteboard. This game normally involves several objects on a tray which are presented to the children. The tray is then covered and the children are asked to close their eyes while you remove an object.

◆   In reality, when this game is played normally it is very difficult to remove an item without the children peeking. Also I find it very difficult to try to show all the objects on a tray when it is tipped at a slight angle without them falling off.

◆   Try inserting images onto a Powerpoint slide and then copy the slide several times.

◆   Remove a different image from each copy of the slide.

◆   This creates a very manageable version of this game. You click through the slides and the children say which image is missing.

Literacy

L3.1, L4.1, L4.2, L5.2

These activities require the children to click and drag boxes to match words to images or construct sentences, paragraphs or longer pieces of text.

Reading and recognizing familiar words, phrases, sentences or paragraphs

109. Click, drag and match

✦   This is a simple activity, but one which the children love to come to the board and do.

✦   Create some 'click-and-drag' boxes on which some have superimposed images and others the matching written word.

✦   The boxes should be jumbled up on the screen.

✦   Invite the children in turn to match up the word and correct image side by side.

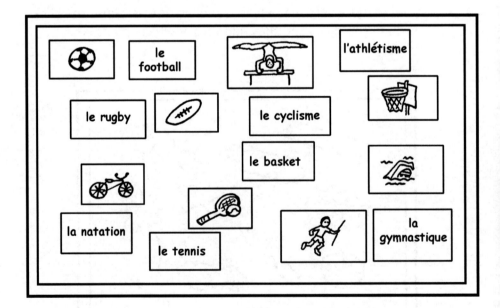

110. **Construct a sentence**

✦ To practise the construction of sentences and to allow the children to experiment and see how language fits together, produce 'click-and-drag' boxes with words which make a sentence.

✦ Invite a child to manipulate the boxes so that the words form a sentence.

✦ These sentences can then be used as a model for writing.

111. **Fill in the blanks**

✦ A variation on activity 110 would be to provide a selection of words in 'click-and-drag' boxes which would fit appropriately in a blank in a sentence.

✦ Ask the children to choose which is the suitable word and say why.

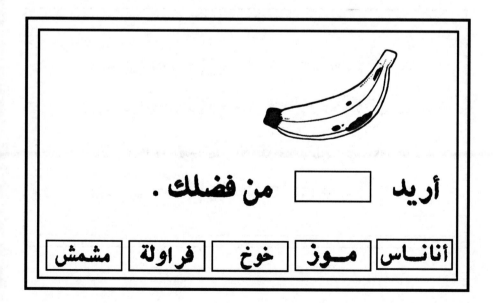

112. **Jumbled paragraph**

✦ For children with more advanced reading skills, a paragraph could be presented from a familiar text. This should be split up and put in 'click-and-drag' boxes, with two or three sentences in each box.

✦ Encourage them to rearrange the boxes in the correct order.

✦ This works well, for example, with a recipe which has a list of instructions or a familiar story or rhyme.

113. **Picture lyrics**

✦ When practising songs or rhymes, try presenting the text with key words and phrases represented by images, so that the children have to read the surrounding text and insert the appropriate words as they sing or recite.

Creativity and imagination

The creativity and imagination of children are two of the best resources in the classroom. With a little guidance from yourself, you can capitalize on these resources.

Communicating orally through language is a performance. In its simplest form this could be an everyday conversation or, more conventionally, drama, song or rhyme. Allowing children to perform through individual interpretation and expression gives ownership of the language to the children and is ultimately more enjoyable. The performance can be live or recorded on video for review and future use. (Check that your school has asked parents for consent to take videos.)

Year 4 children acting out 'Goldilocks and the Three Bears'

Creativity and imagination

Written communication can have many guises. For instance, communication in written form can be illustrated, presented through ICT, written for display, poetic or used in a design description. The possibilities are endless.

This chapter contains a selection of ideas for a variety of topics.

Oracy

O3.1, O3.2, O4.1, O5.4, O6.2

These activities involve children giving a performance of a song, rhyme or piece of drama. There are many very good CDs and tapes of songs in most target languages, including both traditional music and those composed specifically for young language learners. Look out for ones which have a karaoke version to use when performing.

As described in the 'Realia' section, role-play and drama are enhanced by the use of props so it is worth collecting and storing items for this use. I find that drama can become a little boisterous due to the over fertile imaginations of children. For example, simple shopping dialogues can quickly develop into complicated crime scenes involving thieves, the police and frantic chases. Try setting parameters which ensure that the drama is suited to the performing space, especially if you are in a classroom.

The performance could be given to their classmates, to another class or to the rest of the school and parents in an assembly, for example.

Responding to songs, stories and rhymes

114. Listen and clap

✦ To familiarize the children initially with a song, story or rhyme, ask them to clap, stand up or raise their hand each time they hear a particular word or phrase.

115. Actions

✦ Most songs lend themselves to some kind of accompanying physical action which reinforces the children's understanding of their meaning.

✦ If you are ever stuck for an idea, ask the children, they always have plenty.

116. Musical accompaniment

✦ As the children become more confident and join in with a song, story or rhyme, consider if the song can be split into parts or a round.

✦ Instead of a pre-recorded accompaniment, perhaps the children could accompany it playing other instruments.

✦ If the song or rhyme tells a story, try using props to convey the meaning.

117. Clapping games

✦ Using a familiar tune, such as a nursery rhyme, try writing your own words to songs if you are unable to purchase or find an appropriate one.

✦ Alternatively, suggest to the children that they design some clapping actions to a sequence of words. This could be based on clapping games which they do in the playground. I have found children to be very inventive when asked to do this.

118. Happy birthday

✦ Celebrating birthdays is fun for most children. Ask a child if they want the class to sing 'Happy birthday' in the target language on their birthday.

✦ This is a regular feature in my classes. It also provides an opportunity for practising numbers if you ask the class to count out the age of the child.

119. Story-telling

✦ Once children are able to listen to and understand more complex phrases and sentences, try reading and sharing an authentic story or poem.

✦ Ask the children to join in with the reading of the text and create appropriate sound effects and physical responses.

✦ With a little practice and the use of props, a performance of these stories can be very successful and well received in an assembly to the rest of the school.

Giving a short presentation and performing to an audience

120. Counting-in rhymes

✦ Most languages have playground counting-in and out rhymes to find out who will be 'it', the chaser or the one who goes first.

✦ Provide examples of authentic ones in the target language, and then give the children a selection of sounds and words (some of which should be rhyming) and encourage them to make up their own and perform them.

✦ Remember that most of these types of rhymes are often nonsensical so it is not the meaning which is important but the sound.

121. Fashion show

✦ If your learners know the words for items of clothing and colours, ask the children to write a commentary for a fashion show and then perform it using dressing-up clothes.

✦ They will have a lot of fun deciding which clothes to wear as they strut along the catwalk.

122. Weather forecast

✦   With a map as reference, ask the children to pretend that they are on television and presenting a weather forecast.

✦   Cut out weather shapes which can be moved around on the map make it more authentic and interactive. This activity can also be done using an interactive whiteboard.

123. Recipes

✦ As a follow-up to a literacy activity of writing a simple recipe in the target language, ask the children to demonstrate and describe to an audience how to prepare the dish using the actual ingredients.

✦ A fruit salad works well for this.

124. Video presentation

✦ If you have a link with a partner school, give the children a video camera and ask them to create a video presentation about themselves and the school to send to them.

Literacy

L4.4, L5.3, L6.1, L6.4

Most topics lend themselves to a personal response. Displaying children's written work means it can be shared, used for reinforcement of reading skills and, most importantly, be an authentic means of communication. In other words, writing for a purpose.

To achieve some degree of accuracy, the children will need differentiated support in the form of dictionaries or a handout with the vocabulary, which could include images if necessary.

Most written pieces can then be read aloud to the rest of the class and in turn this will help to develop reading and listening skills.

The following activities range from simple labelling of designs to more advanced and creative writing skills.

Writing simple words, phrases and sentences using a reference

125. Photos and captions

✦   Encourage the children to bring in photographs of themselves, their family, house and pets.

✦   Ask them to write captions for the photos, based on a model.

✦   For those children competent in the use of ICT, you could ask them to insert the photos and captions into a presentation to show to the rest of the class.

✦   If you have a link with a school in another country, the presentation could be sent to them as a means of introduction.

126. **Horrible sandwich**

✦ Ask the children to design a delicious or horrible sandwich or pizza based on the vocabulary topic of food.

✦ Cut out sandwich bread shapes. The children can then cut out, colour and stick the sandwich contents between them, labelling each food.

✦ This could be linked to a cross-curricular topic of 'healthy eating'.

127. **Ideal timetable**

✦ For the topic of school, children enjoying designing an ideal timetable for the week.

✦ Give them a blank timetable onto which they can write and draw which subjects they would like to have each day and how often.

128. **Likes and dislikes**

✦ Cut out red heart shapes and ask the children to write in the words for the things which they like and dislike. A heart with a black cross could represent 'dislike'.

✦ Alternatively, write the word for 'like' in the target language and ask the children to write things which they like using a letter from the word for each item. The words should cut through the word 'like' vertically.

129. **Birthday chart**

✦   Create a birthday chart with each month of the year.

✦   Ask the children to write when their birthday is on the chart in the target language.

✦   This will act as a prompt for singing 'Happy birthday' (activity 118).

130. **Menus**

✦   Ask the children to draw, design and label menus for café and restaurant role-plays.

✦   This will also give you an opportunity to discuss the currency of the country.

131. **Fortune teller**

✦   Demonstrate how to make a paper fortune teller (sometimes called a 'Chinese counter' or a 'cootie catcher') and ask the children to write in simple fortunes in the centre such as 'Good luck!' 'You are beautiful', etc.

✦   I find that colours and numbers on the outer layers work well.

Writing sentences using a model, and reading and understanding some detail

132. **Draw a monster**

✦ To practise the vocabulary for parts of the body, ask the children to draw and describe a monster giving them free rein to add as many of each body part as they want and to colour it as they wish.

✦ I have used this activity with a link school. The children describe a monster and send the description to their pen friend.

✦ The pen friends draw the monster according to the description and then return it to the original designer.

✦ This works well and the children love seeing their monsters drawn by someone else.

133. **Wanted!**

✦ Another activity for practising and using vocabulary for parts of the body is to design a 'wanted' poster for an imaginary or, even more fun, a real person in the school.

✦ Display the posters, and don't forget to add a suitable reward for the apprehension of this person!

134. **Poetry**

✦ Simple poetry can be written using familiar vocabulary perhaps supplemented with words from a dictionary.

✦ Try giving the children a simple format to follow such as starting each line alternately with 'Hello' and 'Goodbye'.

✦ You could provide a simple poem in the target language and suggest that the children replace items of vocabulary in the poem with their own words.

135. **Letter to a pen friend**

✦ A link with a school in a country where the target language is spoken provides endless possibilities for the exchange of information, particularly inter-cultural.

✦ One obvious exchange is that of letters between the children. The arrival of letters brings much excitement into the classroom.

✦ Try using a model letter as a starting point for the children to write their own.

136. **Speech bubbles**

✦ Once dialogues and role-plays have been practised, ask the children to write down their conversations by illustrating them in cartoon form with speech bubbles.

✦ Stick men will suffice for those who find drawing cartoon people difficult; humour and interest can be provided through a few extra details.

✦ Alternatively draw the cartoons yourself with empty speech bubbles. Give a selection of language prompts and ask the children to fill in the speech bubbles with appropriate phrases.

✦ A more simplified activity would be to provide the dialogue in the speech bubbles but omit certain words which can be filled in.

137. **Treasure map**

✦ Provide the children with a grid drawn on paper.

✦ Ask the children to draw a treasure island and decide where the treasure is hidden.

✦ Each child writes out instructions for a partner to follow to discover the hiding place.

Index

Activity number

Activity number

Lightning Source UK Ltd.
Milton Keynes UK
UKOW03f0241300913

218141UK00001B/35/P